To those who feel too small to make a difference, I hope you'll find inspiration in the nightly triumph of Earth's tiniest ocean creatures —J.H.

For all the dive buddies I've met, in the ocean and in life —K.L.

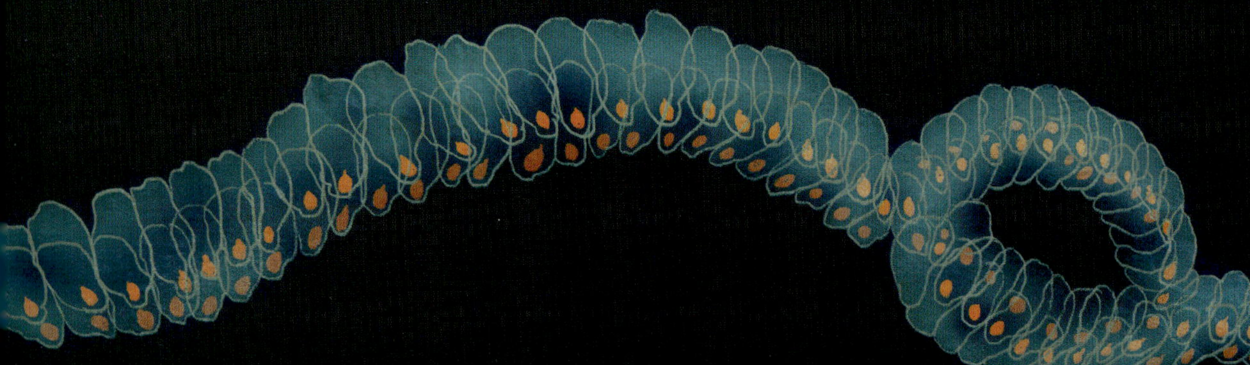

A Note About Size: Zooplankton, phytoplankton, and the sea creatures that eat them are extremely diverse, ranging in size from microscopic to among the largest animals on Earth. To fit this wide range of creatures into the pages of this book, not all species are shown to scale. For size information, please refer to the Monterey Bay Aquarium Research Institute website at www.mbari.org.

Author's acknowledgment: An ocean of thanks to Steven Haddock, PhD, Marine Biologist, Monterey Bay Aquarium Research Institute, for his keen eye in reviewing the text and illustrations. Any remaining errors or inconsistencies are my own.

Millbrook Press™
An imprint of Lerner Publishing Group, Inc.
241 First Avenue North
Minneapolis, MN 55401 USA

For reading levels and more information, look up this title at www.lernerbooks.com.

Diagram on page 32 by Laura K. Westlund.
End paper illustration based on NASA satellite image of Monterey Bay, California.

Designed by Kimberly Morales.
Main body text set in Atelier Sans ITC Std. Typeface provided by International Typeface Corporation.
The illustrations in this book were created digitally.

Library of Congress Cataloging-in-Publication Data

The Cataloging-in-Publication Data for *The Ocean's Heart: The Tiny Creatures Essential to Life* is on file at the Library of Congress.
ISBN 979-8-7656-4346-4 (lib. bdg.)
ISBN 979-8-7656-9974-4 (epub)

Manufactured in Guang Dong, China by Dream Colour Printing
1-1012843-52386-6/18/2025

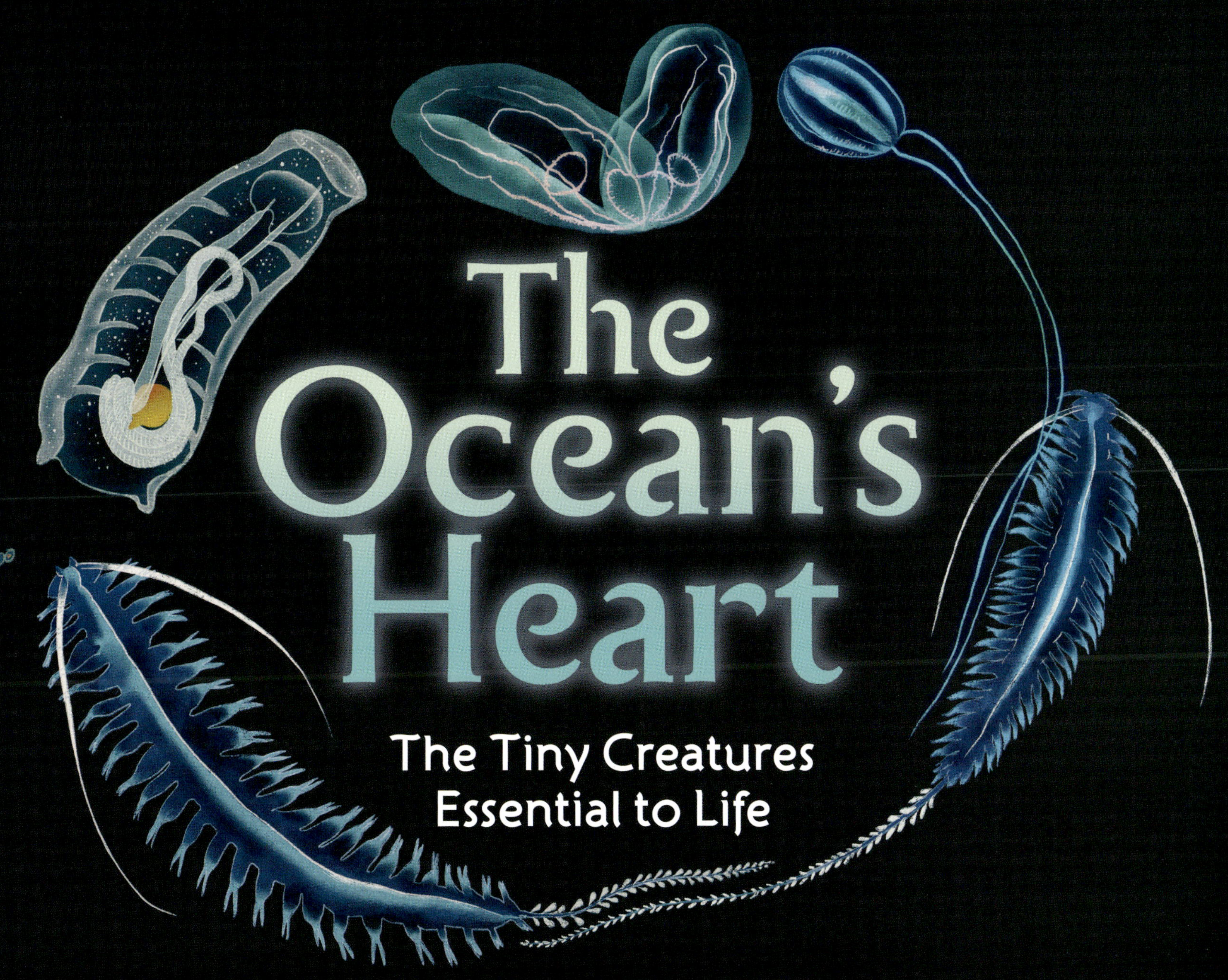

The Ocean's Heart

The Tiny Creatures Essential to Life

Jilanne Hoffmann
illustrated by Khoa Le

Millbrook Press / Minneapolis

Far below the ocean's surface
live tiny, restless creatures
called zooplankton.
They are the ocean's heart.

Behold their strange and glorious beauty!
Most are so small
a thousand may live
in one teaspoon of ocean brine.

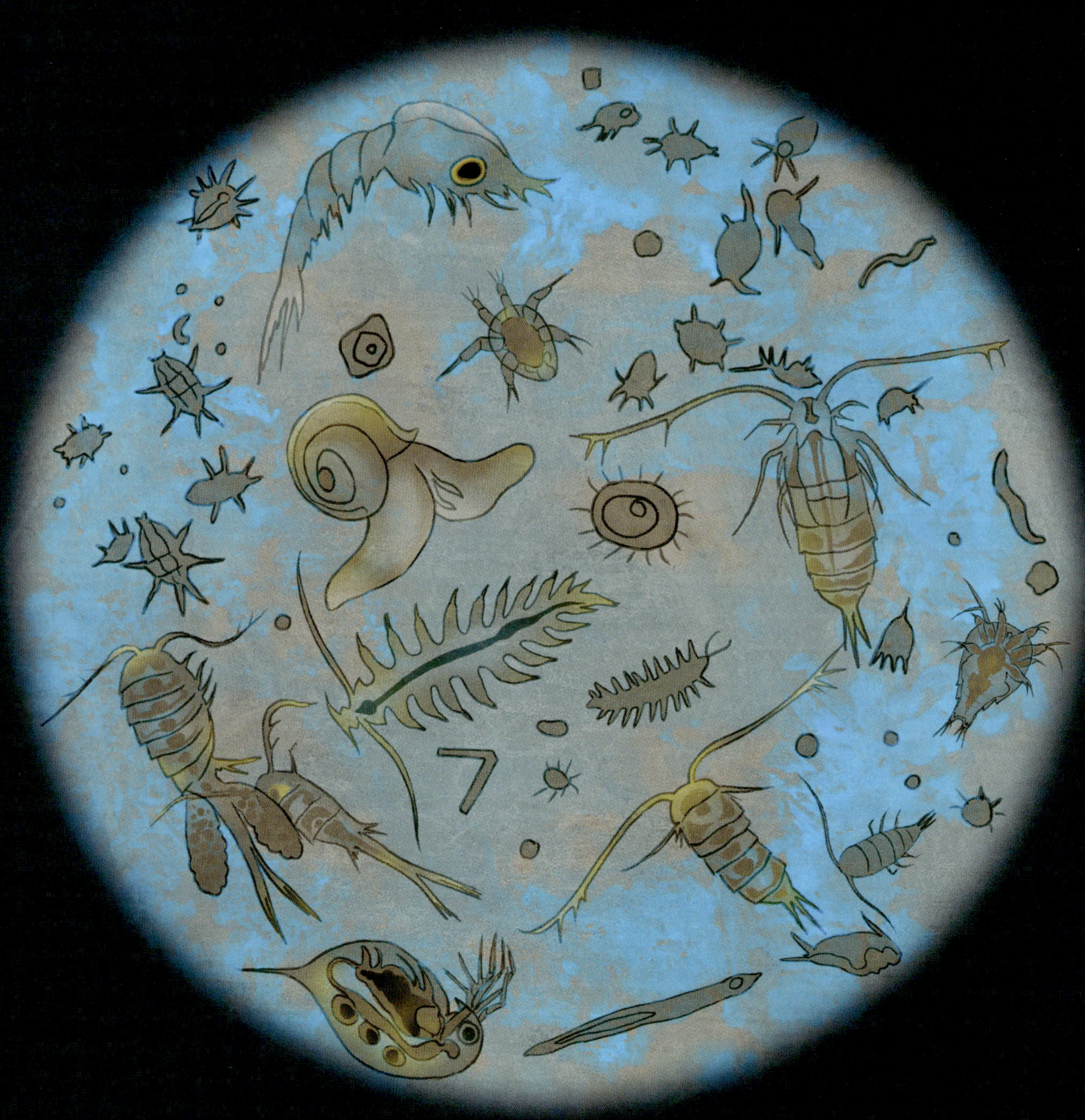

Others, like jellyfish,
can grow quite large.
All of them are plankton,
animals that drift along with currents.

The food they need for their survival—tiny plants—
floats in the shimmering, sunlit surface waters,
far above the zooplankton's home.

Why is their food so far away?

Light is not a friend to zooplankton
because if they can be seen,
they can be caught and eaten.

And so they spend their daylight hours hiding
within the twilight zone,
deep water where it's always dark.

Waiting.

Some eat morsels that drift by.
There is much less here
to satisfy their hunger.
Sometimes they even eat one another.

But when night falls,
they start the race for their survival.

Now *you* must cheer them on their journey.

Why?

Because all life—that means yours too—depends on their success.
If they starve, so will everything that eats them.
That means most ocean creatures,
from the smallest fish to the largest whales,
and all who find their food within its waters.

Our world would be a far more empty place
if we lose zooplankton,
the ocean's heart.

The setting sun reveals tiny, glowing plants in breaking waves
and signals the start of zooplankton's rush to the surface.
It is the largest migration of animals on Earth,
every—single—night.
A teeming mass so large that,
if they were stars,
the ocean would shine more light than any galaxy.

They rise, paddle, and rise.
Rowing, stroking, spinning, spiraling.
Creating currents,
drawing hungry creatures up within their wake.

Predators!

Schools of small, quick fish filter zooplankton
before water passes out their beating gills,
eating on the move.
Squid and shrimp join in.

Many will, in turn, be seized by larger mouths,
biting, tearing, gulping, sifting.
Hunger drives this web of life.

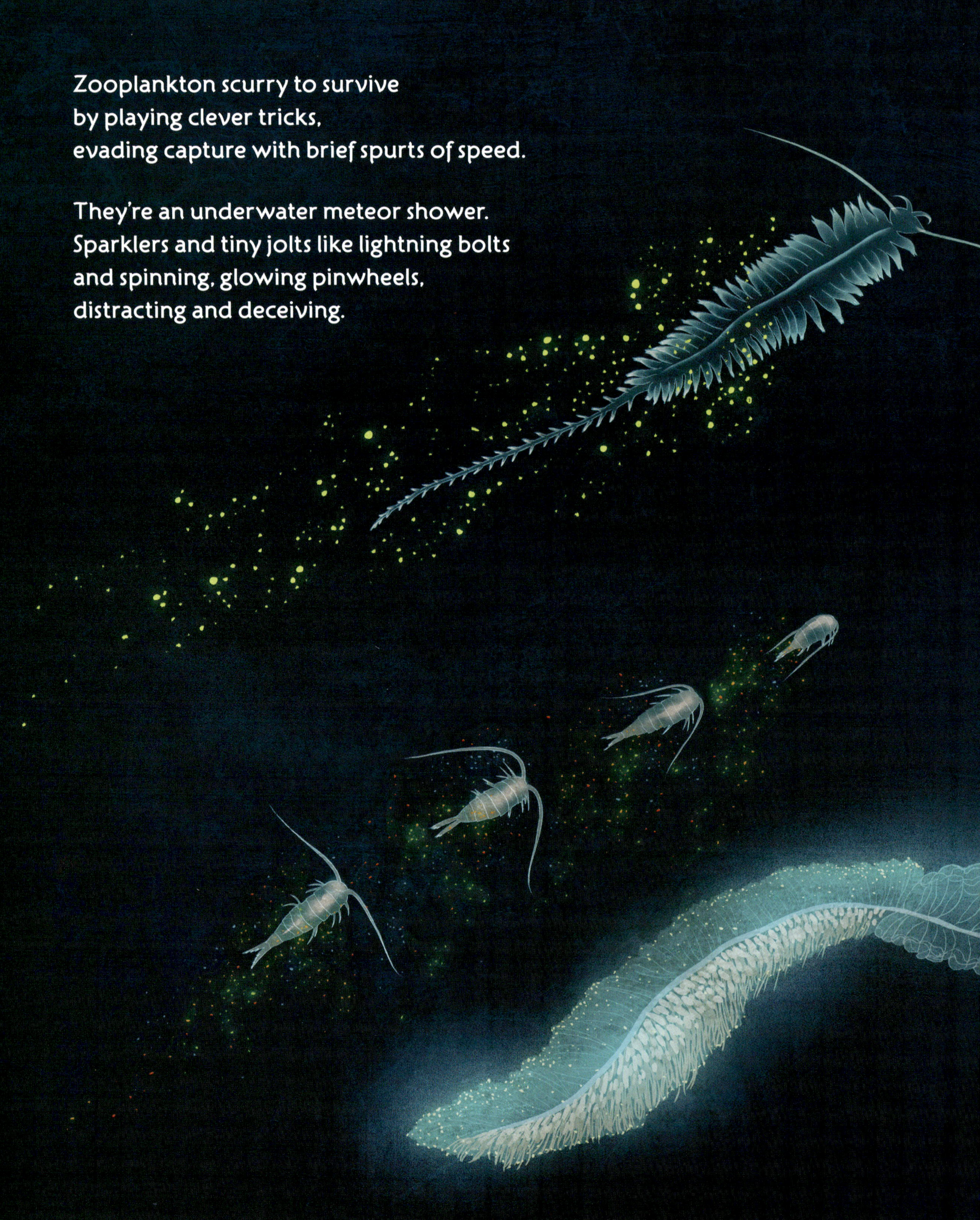

Zooplankton scurry to survive
by playing clever tricks,
evading capture with brief spurts of speed.

They're an underwater meteor shower.
Sparklers and tiny jolts like lightning bolts
and spinning, glowing pinwheels,
distracting and deceiving.

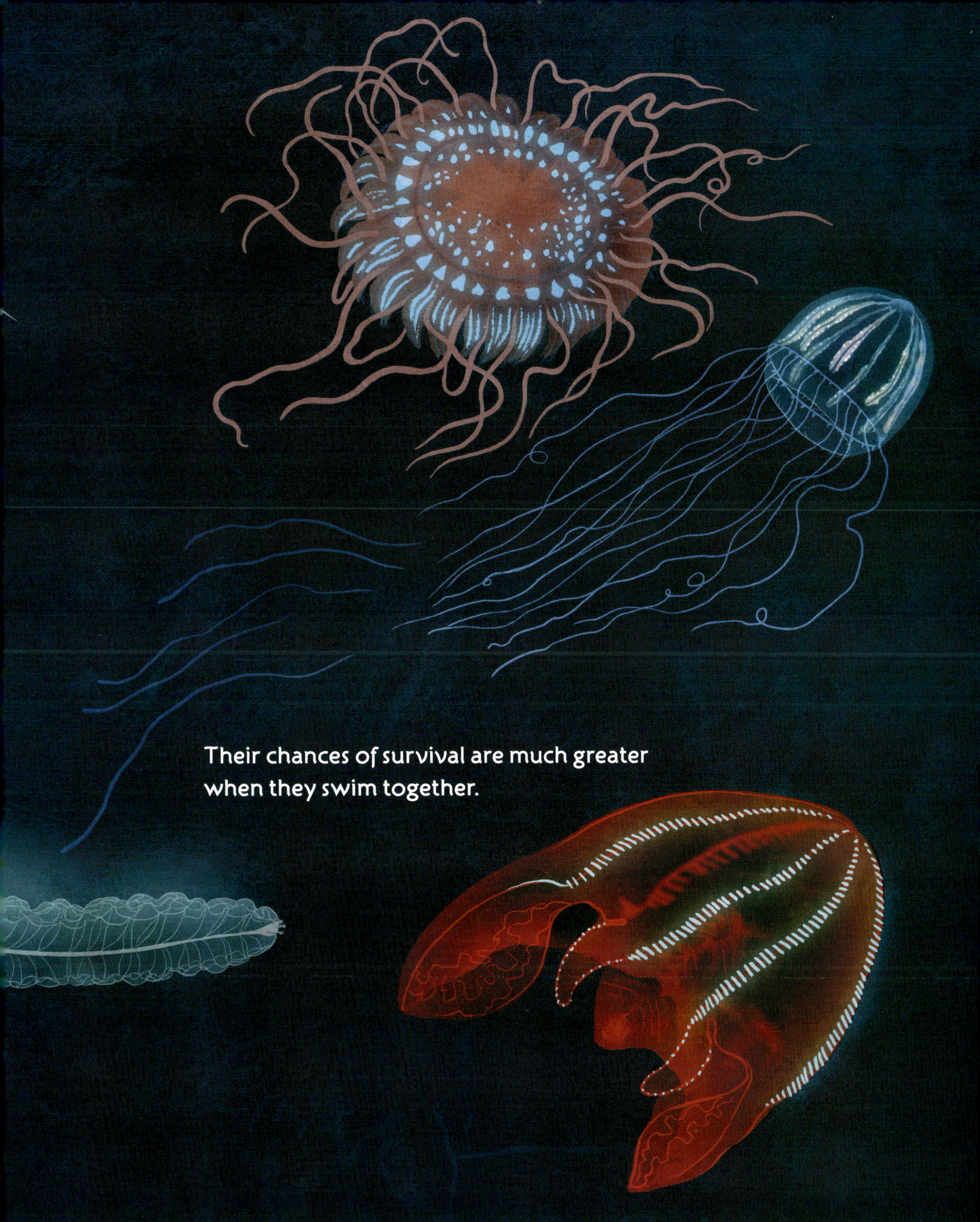

Their chances of survival are much greater when they swim together.

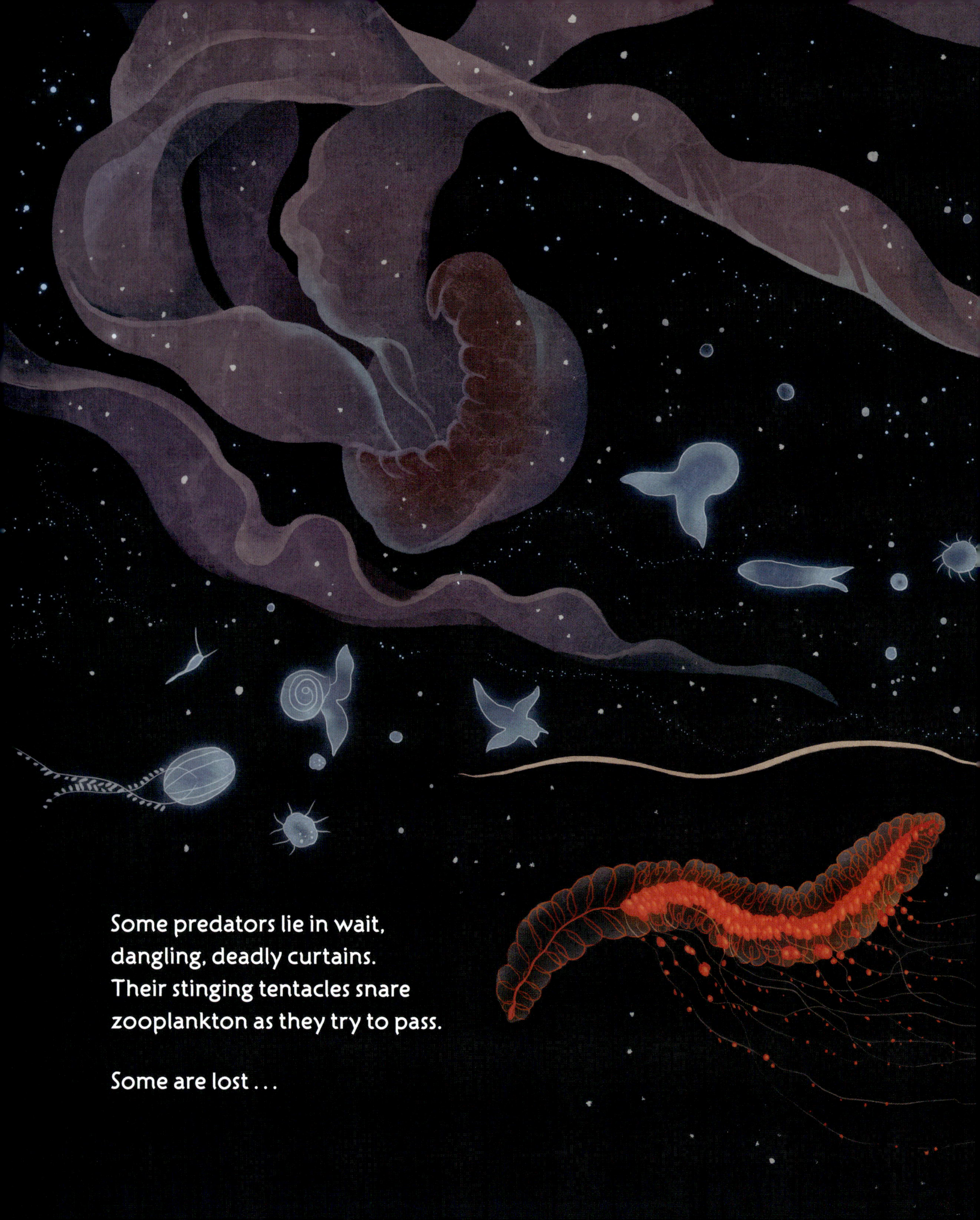

Some predators lie in wait,
dangling, deadly curtains.
Their stinging tentacles snare
zooplankton as they try to pass.

Some are lost . . .

. . . but most still rise, paddle, and rise
up through a falling flurry
of what some call sea snow.
Pieces of animals and plants
no longer living,
snowballing as they fall.
Scraps that feed the scavengers below.

They rise, paddle, and rise.
Until—finally!—
in the middle of the night,
they reach the surface.

You may take a moment here
to savor their success.
But zooplankton have no time to celebrate,
for they must gorge themselves
as if their lives depend on it—
because they do.

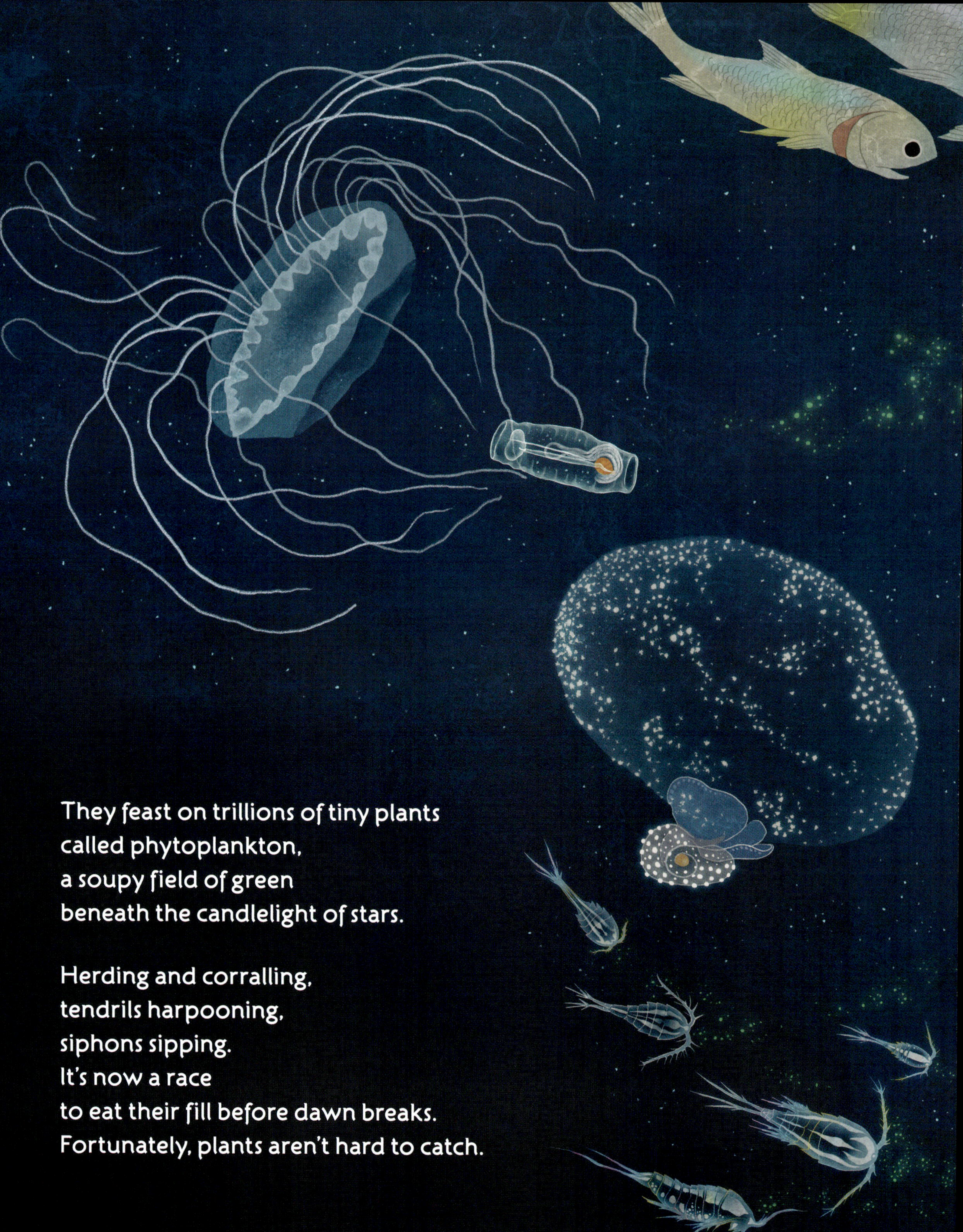

They feast on trillions of tiny plants
called phytoplankton,
a soupy field of green
beneath the candlelight of stars.

Herding and corralling,
tendrils harpooning,
siphons sipping.
It's now a race
to eat their fill before dawn breaks.
Fortunately, plants aren't hard to catch.

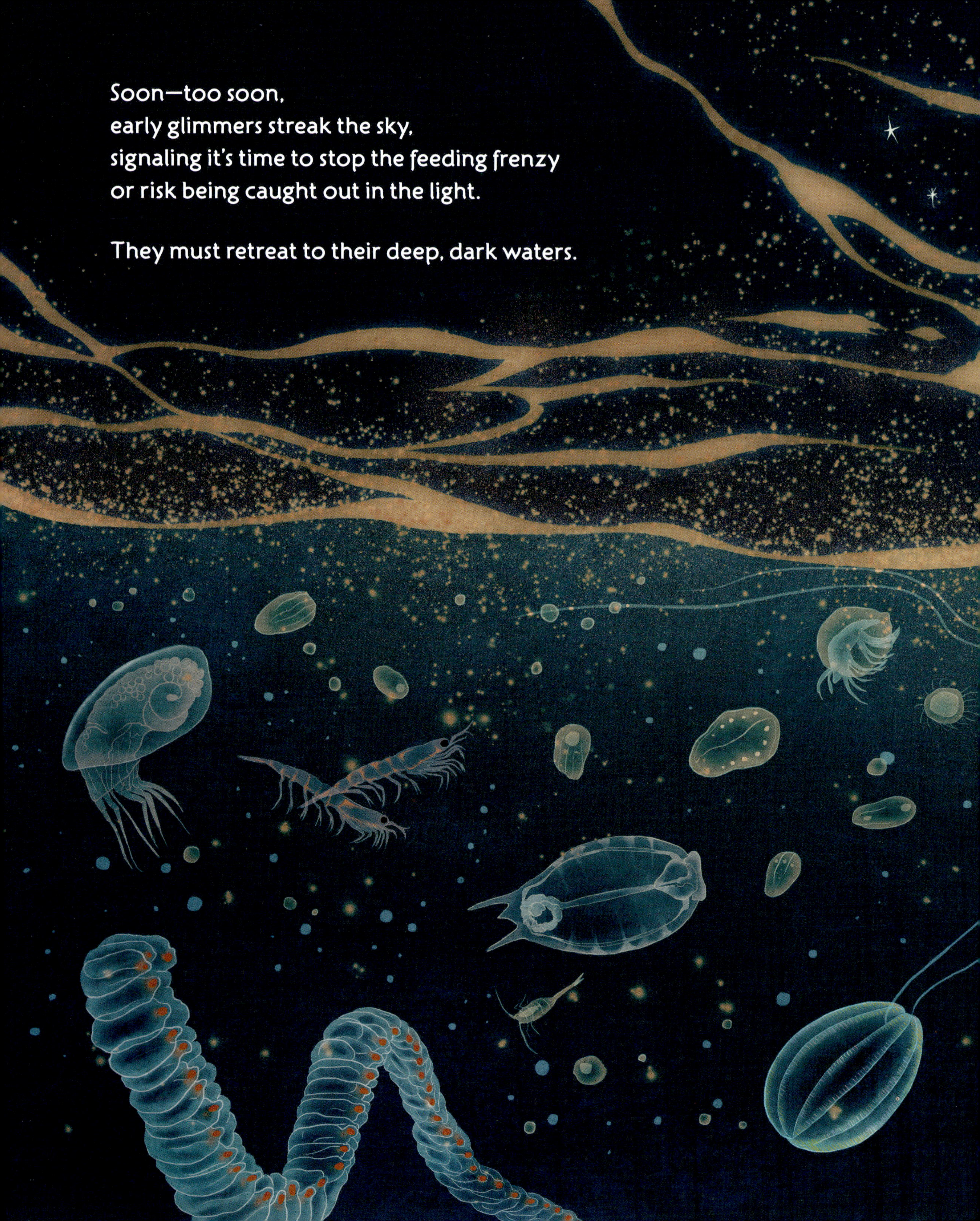

Soon—too soon,
early glimmers streak the sky,
signaling it's time to stop the feeding frenzy
or risk being caught out in the light.

They must retreat to their deep, dark waters.

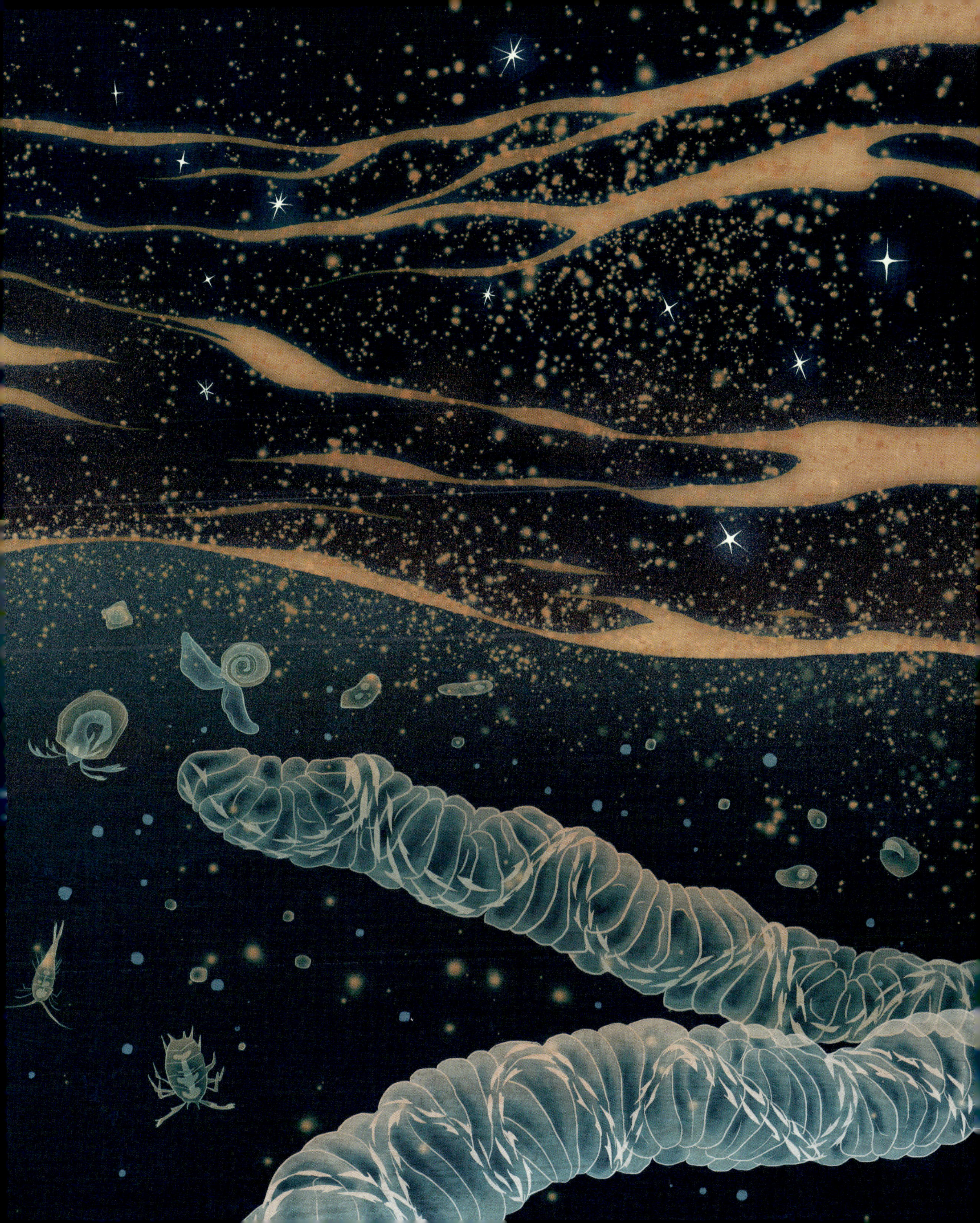

As the sun begins to rise,
zooplankton dive, paddle, and dive,
playing more hide-and-seek
with hunters who are always hungry.
Rowing, stroking, spinning, spiraling,
diving down into the water's depths.

Deeper,

deeper,

deeper.

Zooplankton, the ocean's heart,
the lucky ones who have survived,
hide again in twilight.
Biding their time
until darkness falls once more,
and they rise,
paddle, and rise,

paddle and rise,

paddle and rise,

paddle and rise,

paddle and rise . . .

Zooplankton: The Ocean's Heart

Exactly what are zooplankton? "Zoo" means animal, and "plankton" means drifter. So, according to their name, zooplankton are animals that drift in the water. They got this name long before scientists realized that, in fact, they don't *only* drift with the current, they also swim to make their nightly journey to and from the ocean's surface.

Tens of thousands of zooplankton species have been identified, and scientists estimate that tens of thousands more have yet to be discovered. Although zooplankton live in both saltwater and freshwater, this book focuses on those in the ocean. Specifically, the illustrations show creatures found in the Monterey Bay National Marine Sanctuary, which is located off the central California coast in the Pacific Ocean.

Zooplankton are concentrated in the ocean's Twilight Zone, 650 to 3,300 feet (200 to 1,000 m) below the surface, where little light reaches and food is scarce. About 98 percent of zooplankton are microscopic, meaning they're so small you can only see them clearly with a microscope. Some zooplankton are floating eggs and larval stages of much larger ocean creatures. Some, such as krill and jellyfish, grow large enough to be seen with the naked eye; however, they're still considered plankton, because they continue to drift on ocean currents. When zooplankton grow into speedy swimmers (such as fish or squid), or into animals that live on the ocean floor (such as sea stars or crabs), they're no longer considered plankton.

Copepods outnumber all other zooplankton. They're among the most plentiful animals on Earth, so it's not surprising they're nicknamed "the insects of the sea." Some copepods can swim 295 feet (90 m) in an hour, the equivalent of a human swimming 50 miles (81 km) per hour. But they tend to use their speed in short bursts to escape predators or to ambush prey. Each one may eat nearly four hundred thousand phytoplankton (floating plantlike organisms) in a single day!

I call zooplankton the ocean's "heart" because they act as a vital organ and circulatory system for the ocean. They take in nutrients when they eat phytoplankton, and then they pass those nutrients along to the creatures that eat them.

Zooplankton's Nightly Journey

Around the world, the ocean's zooplankton are drifting in the Twilight Zone, rising in the darkness, dining through the night, or diving back down as dawn breaks. Think of it as zooplankton doing "the wave" around the world, a bit like sports fans in a stadium.

The journey to the surface is only the halfway mark of their full marathon that, to a human, would be like swimming 250 miles (402 km) each night. Some zooplankton are motionless in between power strokes that send them surging through the water. This makes them harder for predators to see and catch. Many feed while swimming, constantly dog paddling, spinning, or beating their whiplike cilia (hairlike structures that help them eat and move through water). Most zooplankton luminesce (make light using chemicals). Some flash brightly, some spew glowing clouds, and some mimic the light made by other creatures to lure prey or startle and confuse predators. If you'd like to see zooplankton in action, the resources on the following page offer incredible photos and videos.

Throughout the ocean, zooplankton and their predators travel through sea snow, particles of poop and dead plants and animals that slowly fall toward the ocean floor. The scientific term for this flurry is "marine snow." It provides essential food to scavengers on the ocean floor as well as to creatures that swim through it, including zooplankton.

Zooplankton migration is so massive that it creates its own currents. When zooplankton swim upward, they pull down surface water that has absorbed heat from the atmosphere. And as they swim back down to the Twilight Zone, cold, nutrient-rich water flows upward to feed phytoplankton on the surface. This mixing, vital to the health of all ocean life, helps regulate Earth's climate and is as powerful as the currents caused by wind and tides.

Phytoplankton: The Foundation of the Ocean's Food Web

If zooplankton are the "beating heart" of a healthy ocean, phytoplankton can be thought of as the ocean's "lungs." They must live at or near the ocean's surface because they, like plants on land, use sunlight to make their food (sugar) through photosynthesis. In the process, they absorb up to 2.2 billion tons (2,000,000,000 mt) of carbon dioxide annually, and they release more oxygen than all land-based plants (including trees) on Earth. So you can give thanks to phytoplankton each time you take a breath.

During photosynthesis, the carbon (a basic building block of all life on Earth) from carbon dioxide becomes part of the phytoplankton, just like the food you eat becomes part of you. That carbon is then absorbed by zooplankton as they eat phytoplankton. When zooplankton swim downward, they take the absorbed carbon with them. This "carbon sink" helps to slow global warming by removing carbon dioxide (a greenhouse gas) from the atmosphere.

A Tangled Food Web

The ocean is an eat-or-be-eaten world. This diagram presents only a tiny sample of ocean creatures that feed on plants or one another. Arrows show the energy and nutrient flow from prey to predator. Arrows that loop back indicate those that eat their own kind. Zooplankton and some larger creatures, such as crabs and sea stars, also feed on marine snow. Decomposers, such as bacteria, recycle nutrients from marine snow back into the ocean water, where they can be taken up by other plants and animals.

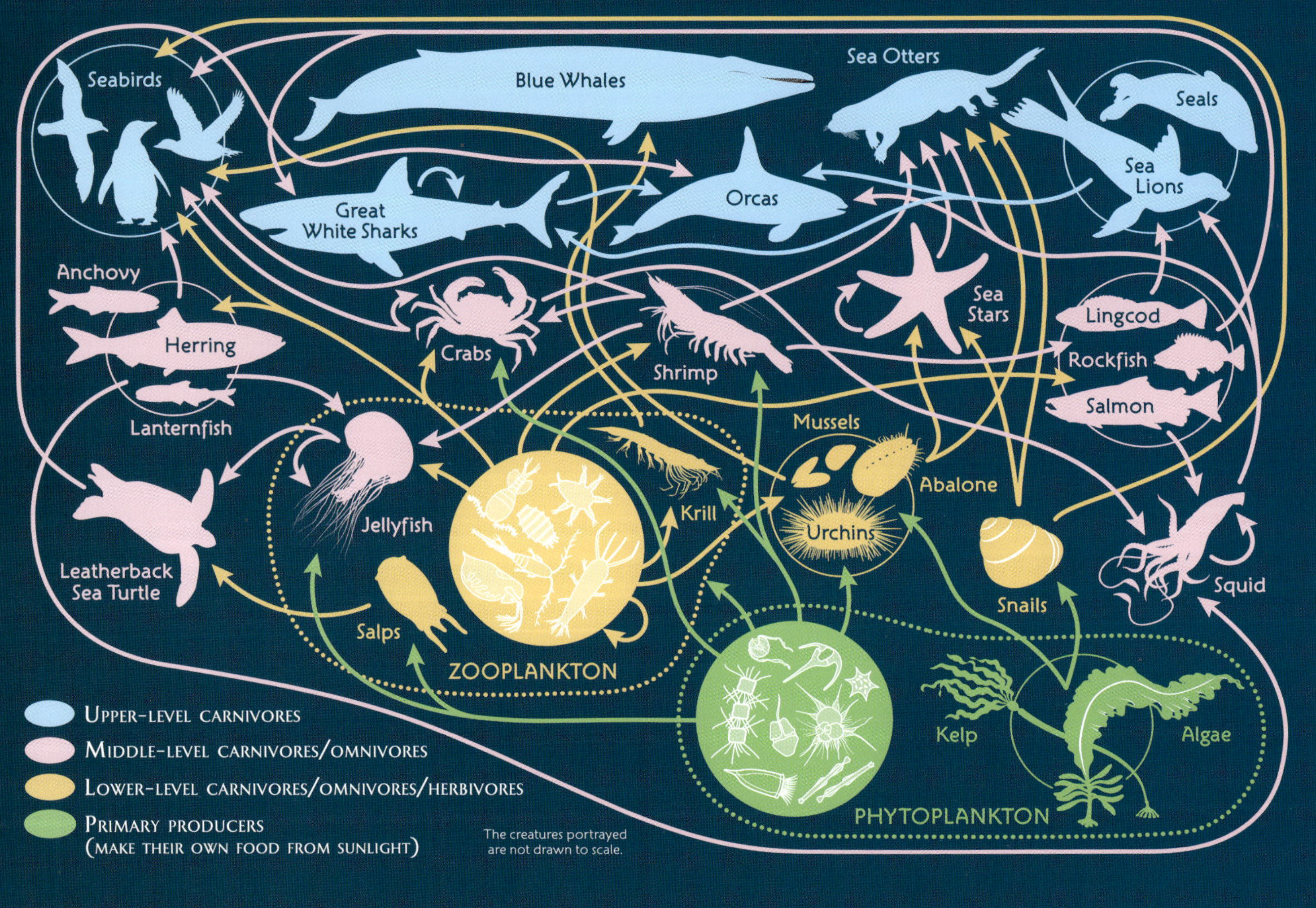

Plankton in Danger

Scientists estimate that phytoplankton populations have fallen by as much as 40 percent since the 1950s, possibly due to climate change. As the number of phytoplankton drops, so does the number of zooplankton that eat them. In some cases, less desirable phytoplankton are overrunning the kinds that zooplankton prefer. Think of it as going to a restaurant night after night where none of the food on the menu is what you can eat, or where there's not enough food to feed every customer. You could end up starving!

Human-caused disruptions, such as mining the ocean floor for minerals, and industrial trawling (a habitat-destroying type of fishing that scrapes the ocean floor), stir up sediment, making seawater cloudy. This can disrupt the way zooplankton and other sea creatures find food and reproduce. Plastic pollution also threatens zooplankton, because they may accidentally eat tiny plastic particles instead of nutritious food. Mining, trawling, and plastic pollution threaten the entire ocean's food web.

You Can Help Zooplankton!

Here are some ways you can help protect the ocean and its creatures.

- Conservation starts with caring. Start a "Zooplankton Are Deep" awareness week at your school, and collect donations to support ocean research and conservation organizations. See author's website for details.
- If you live near the ocean, take part in beach clean-ups.
- Reduce the amount of plastic you use. All plastic is bad for the ocean, and plastic bags harm sea turtles who mistakenly eat them, thinking they're food.
- Write letters to your representatives, asking them to support bans on deep-sea mining and industrial trawling. Sending letters as a group will amplify the power of your voice!

Selected Resources

Books

Brunelle, Lynn. *Life After Whale: The Amazing Ecosystem of a Whale Fall*. Illustrated by Jason Chin. Holiday House, 2024.

Haddock, Steven, and Sönke Johnsen. *The Radiant Sea: Color and Light in the Underwater World*. Abrams, 2025.

Hoyt, Erich. *Planktonia: The Nightly Migration of the Ocean's Smallest Creatures*. Firefly Books, 2022.

Newman, Patricia. *Planet Ocean: Why We All Need a Healthy Ocean*. Photographs by Annie Crawley. Millbrook Press, 2021.

Siems, Annika, and Wolfgang Dreyer. *Into the Deep: An Exploration of Our Oceans*. Prestel, 2019.

Williams, Lily. *If Sharks Disappeared*. Roaring Brook Press, 2017.

Websites

Monterey Bay Aquarium Research Institute (MBARI)
https://www.mbari.org/education/more-resources

NOAA Ocean Exploration
https://oceanexplorer.noaa.gov/edu/doep/welcome.html

Woods Hole Oceanographic Institution
https://www.whoi.edu/what-we-do/educate/k-12-students-and-teachers